I0060461

# WHALE HUNTERS WISDOM SERIES
## Volume IV

# THE WHALE HUNTING CULTURE

Engage Your Entire Company
in Business Development

## Dr. Barbara Weaver Smith
### and The Whale Hunters

**The Whale Hunters**
**BIGGER DEALS**
**BIGGER CUSTOMERS**

# Whale Hunters Wisdom Series

### By Dr. Barbara Weaver Smith
and The Whale Hunters

Volume I

**Mind of a Hunter:** Cultivate Your Company's Strategic Sales Mentality

Volume II

**The Hunt:** Strengthen Your Sales Process to Accelerate Business Growth

Volume III

**Riding the Whale:** Adapt Your Sales Strategies to Close Big Deals

Volume IV

**The Whale Hunting Culture:** Engage Your Entire Company in Business Development

info@thewhalehunters.com

www.thewhalehunters.com
© 2007-2016 The Whale Hunters, Inc.

ISBN: 978-0-9975379-1-8

Published in the United States of America by The Whale Hunters, Inc.

The Whale Hunters
3054 East Bartlett Place
Chandler, AZ 85249
www.thewhalehunters.com
info@thewhalehunters.com

480.584.4012

# Preface

Aimed at owners and executives seeking explosive growth for their companies, the *Whale Hunters Wisdom* series offers explanations, tools, personal anecdotes and real life examples to guide you in scouting, hunting, and harvesting "whales," those accounts 10 to 20 times larger than your current average account.

The Whale Hunters Process™ is derived from our study of how the Inuit people of far northwestern Alaska hunted whales. Their story is one of indomitable courage and persistence. A small team of people ventured out into icy waters in a sealskin boat during the dark days of early Spring to capture and then land and harvest the biggest mammal on earth. Their story has the power of truth, and we have great respect and admiration for the Inuit. The dangerous hunt demanded tremendous courage, a special boat and tools, and a ritual that ensured the hunters and villagers would be successful. Why did the whale hunters risk their lives? **One whale will feed the village for an entire year.**

The Whale Hunters, Inc. is a strategic sales and business development company. We teach a process to develop a fast-growth culture within your company. This permanent process integration requires a defined strategy with clear steps, teamwork, defined responsibilities, and a common understanding that the village survives because it hunts.

Through The Whale Hunters Process™, your company will be positioned for explosive growth that can be managed consistently as you land and support whale-sized accounts. Learn more by visiting our website, www.thewhalehunters.com, where you may register to receive the *Whale Hunters Wisdom* newsletter. It's absolutely free.

info@thewhalehunters.com

www.thewhalehunters.com

# The Whale Hunters Process™

## *A proven, nine-phase process for transforming sales development*

Whale Hunting creates a disciplined sales culture in your company that allows you to optimize your ability to land and harvest large accounts. This dramatic shift in thinking and practice precipitates explosive growth of your company's revenues and market position.

**Scouting** guides you to know, seek and harpoon whales whose business will be ideal for you. It all starts with knowing who you're hunting, with a focus on market and sales research and the creation of a target filter.

Harpoon     Know

Scout

Seek

Celebrate     Beach

Harvest

Sew     Ride

Honor

Hunt

Capture

**Hunting** focuses on communicating with, presenting to, and securely closing your ideal whale accounts. Our method of progressive discovery and disclosure relies on critical questions at each step of the hunt.

**Harvesting** brings sales and operations departments together in an integrated process to ensure you harvest your whale effectively, efficiently and harmoniously. It includes key account management and growing new business with your best accounts.

V

info@thewhalehunters.com

# Table of Contents

info@thewhalehunters.com         www.thewhalehunters.com

© 2007-2016 The Whale Hunters, Inc.

# Introduction

For the Inuit whale hunters, the hunt was surely a wonderful experience, oft-discussed until the stories became legend. The bitter cold. The size of the whale. The size of the waves. The precise placement of the harpoon. The long ride through treacherous, icy waters. The successes and near-failures.

Once the hunt was over and the whale was beached, was this the time for the village to go home and rest? Not by a long shot! Now was the time for the real work to begin. The whale had to be harvested, and the entire village had to take part. The consequences of a poorly-done harvest would negate all the efforts of the hunts. And all the great stories would not feed the village through the next long, cold winter.

So it is with companies for whom a whale hunt has been successful. You have the contract signed. Everyone is pleased.

Now the task of fulfilling the contract goes to everyone within your company. You must have a culture within your company that allows you to take full advantage of all the benefits the whale provides. This is not the glamorous part of the whale hunt, but it is among the most important. The actions taken by your company throughout the harvesting process will dictate whether you can be successful hunting whales and whether you can hope to hunt more in the future.

Imagine, for example, a situation in which the Inuit villagers fought over which family would get the best cuts of meat. In their anger, several families storm off, only to leave parts of the whale to rot in the sun. Or imagine that a herd of caribou happened by at the same time as the whale was beached. Several of the best hunters of the village chased after the caribou, and the whale carcass was washed back out to sea with the outgoing tide. Imagine the recriminations and fear that would prevail over the village as the next winter threatened to leave it starving.

The entire village must begin the harvest as soon as the contract is signed. Volume Four in the *Whale Hunters Wisdom* series offers methods to ensure that your company culture is optimal for a plentiful harvest.

www.thewhalehunters.com

*Whether entrepreneurial, internally competitive, bureaucratic, or fast-growth, all company cultures have their upsides and downsides. But only fast-growth companies are best positioned for success in whale hunting.*

4

# Fast-Growth Culture

The Whale Hunters work with fast-growth companies to accelerate their ability to sell and serve large, complex accounts.

*What do we mean by "fast growth"?*

A fast-growth company is one with a high level of collaboration among employees who believe that the resources are adequate and effectively deployed. Collaboration is how easily people can share knowledge and work together for a common purpose. Resources are the money, time, personnel, and technology to accomplish the company's goals.

Your company's culture is driven by the interaction of these two key variables.

Clearly the levels of collaboration and resources vary widely across organizations; and, within any given organization, across time. But by considering these two variables, it's possible to characterize a specific organization's culture in one of the following ways:

**Entrepreneurial.** High energy and fervent belief define the typical start-up culture. Clients drive decisions and the organization uses a team-based decision-making process. Leaders and employees behave like stakeholders; job responsibilities are fluid; and a "can-do" attitude prevails. Money is tight and hours are long, but the team of believers accomplishes great things and celebrates group success. However, unless they work to build replicable processes, entrepreneurial companies run the risk of inefficiencies and expending key resources in too many directions.

**Internally Competitive.** Left to its own devices, the entrepreneurial culture becomes internally competitive over time. Introducing a more formal management structure and increasing divisions of labor create a perceived need for line managers to compete for resources and recognition. Although some managers see competition as high performance, collaboration always suffers as competition increases. Internally competitive companies are vulnerable to external threats and run the risk of fighting fires rather than anticipating new directions. The energy required to regain that entrepreneurial spirit is exhausting.

**Bureaucratic.** The internally competitive culture can even out over time if the company continues to acquire sufficient financial and human resources. Bureaucracies are stable and therefore confident. They are also slow-moving. Bureaucratic companies run the risk of missed opportunities because of slow response time and resistance to change. Processes become stagnant; and there is not enough collaboration to permit agility and market readiness.

**Fast-Growth.** The fast-growth company integrates the best of an entrepreneurial spirit with the desire to implement reliable processes that are continually reviewed and improved. In the fast-growth company, decision-making occurs at all levels, yet there is a clear escalation process. Change is embedded as a core competency. Leaders and employees understand how to balance quick reaction time with a sense of overall control that reduces panic and builds confidence. Striking the delicate balance between resources and collaboration levels requires conscious and sustained effort. But the results are worth it: fast-growth companies are best positioned for success in their whale hunting endeavors.

## What type of culture exists within your company?

6

# Reflection

Here is an illustration of the four types of culture described in this chapter. Where is your company in the culture cube? Seek input from your team—see if everyone agrees.

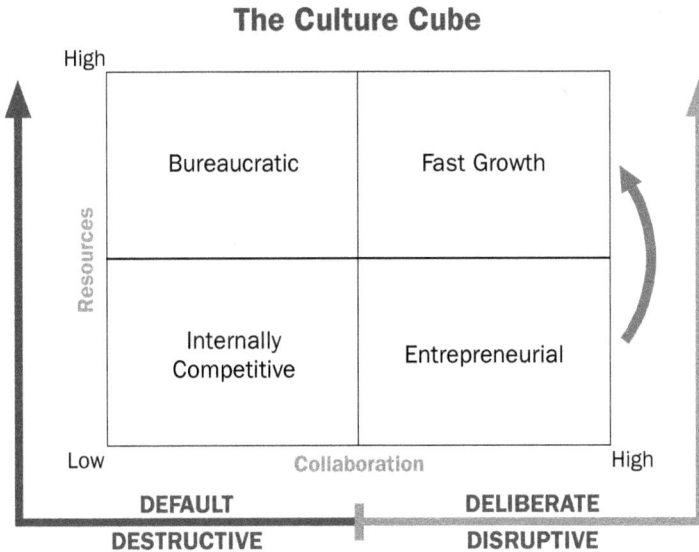

## The Culture Cube

| | Bureaucratic | Fast Growth |
|---|---|---|
| **Resources** High | | |
| Low | Internally Competitive | Entrepreneurial |

Collaboration: Low — High

DEFAULT     DELIBERATE

DESTRUCTIVE     DISRUPTIVE

What evidence supports your analysis of your company's culture as it is today?

_____

_____

_____

_____

_____

7

# Action

Identify up to five steps your company could take to move towards a fast growth culture or to improve (if you are already set up for fast growth). Explain how to do each step and recruit a champion.

| Step to Take | Specific Actions | Champion |
| --- | --- | --- |
|  |  |  |
|  |  |  |
|  |  |  |

8

*No amount of "busy-ness" should ever overrule your business. Keep your eyes on the work as well as on the opportunities on the horizon. A target filter will help you prioritize those opportunities to greatest advantage.*

9

# The Village is TOO Busy for Whales!

Yogi Berra had many malapropisms that made him famous and funny. One of my favorites is, "That place is so busy, nobody goes there anymore!" Like the too-crowded restaurant, a village convinced that it can't hunt new whales because it is too busy with current responsibilities dooms itself to long-term difficulty and possible failure.

In fact, sometimes we are invited to work with a company whose employees are busy pushing whales off the beach and back into the Bering Sea!

What are the symptoms of a village in overload mode?

See if any of these sound familiar:

- "I'm so busy right now; I can't possibly put anything new on my plate."

- "You can never get Joe to come to meetings because he is so busy putting out fires."

- "Somebody has got to tell the sales department to slow down, or we will begin to lose people from overwork!"

- "If we are not careful, something is going to slip through the cracks, and then who are they going to blame?"

- "All we seem to do around here is meet and try to carve up the work differently so that it will get done. What we really need is a bunch more people."

10

Capacity is a difficult balancing act for a company trying to grow rapidly. It is hard to anticipate with accuracy the resources that you will need for new business while maintaining profitability and operational integrity. In essence, leadership is working with equations that have too many variables including new sales, current support, market conditions, client satisfaction, and long-term goals. It makes the head swim to consider how many ways you can get this calculus wrong and how few ways you can get it right.

Yet a company too busy to take on new customers today is doomed to have no new customers tomorrow. A company must have eyes looking out for new opportunities as well as eyes looking down and doing the work. Without eyes looking both places, you will most assuredly miss the whales… and perhaps the caribou, and the trout, and everything else it takes to keep your village alive.

Ideally, your company creates a target filter to sort the work and consider it strategically (see Volume I: Mind of a Hunter). Issues to consider include resources, profitability, long-term product development, and other key metrics specific to your business. Compare your opportunities against this filter, and figure out what items should be shelved, delayed, or acted upon.

Be guarded with the precious resource of your firm's time and only take on work that makes sense for you to do. Build a strategic plan that identifies the "crunch points" at which new capacity needs to be sourced. Consider whether such capacity should be accomplished through technology, additional employees, realigned resources, outsource partners, and/or other creative options.

The Whale Hunters assist our clients to build target filters for accurate decision-making. When considering the variables, a good filter will manage the "now," anticipate the "future," and balance both against corporate goals. Sometimes organizations really are incapable of taking on new clients; but more often, they simply need to identify and try to eliminate those low-value activities that keep the village "too busy" and thus stand in the way of new whales.

Visit our website now to claim your free infographic How Team Selling Lands Bigger Customers, Bigger Deals!
http://thewhalehunters.com/infographic1

www.thewhalehunters.com
info@thewhalehunters.com

# Reflection

Is your company in overload mode?

What do you hear, directly or indirectly, about work load? If you don't hear, ask key people what they hear.

Identify five statements that reflect your village's current perception of their work.

1.

2.

3.

4.

5.

# Action

With your team, review your strategic plan for the next year to three years. [Don't have a plan? It's time to make one! Email us if you want our recommendation for a simple, powerful plan].

1. Have you shared a strategic plan with your team? If not, do that.

2. Is your team spending time on activities that are not moving toward your strategic goals? If yes, how will you redirect their efforts?

3. Does your team believe that if they take on new work, you will see that they have new resources if needed to get that work done? In other words, do they trust you to be fair with the new revenue?

A fast-growth culture is a belief system, a state of mind, a perception. If your people are afraid that a big new customer will overwhelm them with new work, they will not share your enthusiasm. Work with your village to get over "being too busy."

www.thewhalehunters.com
© 2007-2016 The Whale Hunters, Inc.

info@thewhalehunters.com

> *Oh, we can't do that NOW! No, we're too*
> *_____, or we're not _____*
> *enough, or we have to _____*
> *first. Really? If you can't get over those*
> *hurdles, you'll never reach your goals.*

15

# What Are You Waiting For?

Every single day we talk to leaders of companies who say they want to implement a strategy and process to accelerate their growth. Some of those leaders move ahead aggressively to pursue their growth plan strategy, but many do not. Why is that? Why delay action on an agenda that the leader has decided is <u>important</u> and <u>appropriate</u> and <u>aligned</u> with the company's strategic vision?

I'm talking about companies whose goal (often in the form of their strategic plan) calls for doubling or tripling their revenue in this year or the next. That is an enormous goal, one that a company is unlikely to reach without a very serious plan of action. Still, many leaders choose to delay implementing a strategy even after they have decided it is the right strategy to achieve their goals. What's getting in their way? Here are the top five excuses:

- **Time.** I know this is critically important to our growth, but we simply don't have time right now. Or, I don't have time to take leadership of this initiative. In a month or two when I can get X-Y-Z off my plate, then maybe I will have time (for my most important new business strategy!)

- **Money.** Yes, we intend to grow our business by two times or three times our current revenue in the next couple of years. But, please understand, we don't have the cash flow to invest in a strategic initiative at this time. We will just have to work harder on our pipeline.

- **Personnel.** Yes, we really want to get going on this initiative to grow our business. But we are currently thinking about hiring a new director of business development (or sales professional or sales manager). We can't

16

get started without that person on board. Or, one of our key employees recently left our company. We really can't move forward until we figure out how to replace that person/position.

- **Culture.** My team really isn't ready to buy into this strategy. I need time to work with them and bring them on board. We need to have some internal meetings to see if I can get them to agree to what we need to do next.

- **Unique Circumstance.** I understand that Whale Hunting has been successful in many companies over time. But you don't understand my business and how it is completely different from any other business that you've worked with. We have to manage a totally different set of circumstances and we face a totally different set of challenges.

So, how do any of these observations relate to you and your business objectives? It's certainly not about whether or not you engage The Whale Hunters. But it IS about whether you move your company forward, right now, on a path to achieve the growth goals and metrics that you have set out.

If you have an agenda to double or triple your growth in, say, two years, maybe you've already let Q1 get away from you if you haven't cleared your plate to make this your Number 1 initiative (time excuse).

Now you're down to 7 quarters, not 8. And if you didn't do anything in Q1 to invest in any new ways of prospecting, you're down to 6 quarters (money excuse).

17

If you are postponing important strategic initiatives until you have new people on board, you are down to at least 5 quarters (personnel excuse).

If you don't have your team on board and haven't really started to bring them on board, you are suddenly down to only ONE YEAR to implement a two year strategy. Plus, if this year doesn't bring significant growth, your growth goals for next year are at least double your goal for the current year (culture excuse).

Finally, in terms of unique circumstances, I do understand that every company is unique and that your needs and objectives differ from every other company. But the more you can identify your unique circumstance with the success-and-failure parameters of other small and midsize businesses, the more you can benefit from a body of knowledge and practice that will apply to you at least 90% of the time if not more.

The clock is ticking. In this economy, if you do not feel a sense of urgency, it's likely you will be left behind. Whatever excuses are in the way of your moving ahead, work hard today to eliminate them.

Visit our website now to claim your free infographic How Team Selling Lands Bigger Customers, Bigger Deals!
http://thewhalehunters.com/infographic1

# Reflection

Make a list of initiatives or activities you really need to start but haven't begun yet. Then prioritize your list as to each initiative's strategic importance.

RANK    INITIATIVE

——    _____

——    _____

——    _____

——    _____

——    _____

——    _____

——    _____

——    _____

——    _____

——    _____

——    _____

——    _____

19

www.thewhalehunters.com
© 2007-2016 The Whale Hunters, Inc.

# Action

Based on understanding our ocean and our rivers in the ocean, here are five actions we can take to improve our marketing and/or sales collateral, including our website:

| Step | Activity | Responsible Person | Due Date |
|------|----------|--------------------|----------|
|      |          |                    |          |
|      |          |                    |          |
|      |          |                    |          |
|      |          |                    |          |
|      |          |                    |          |

20

*Your car will last a lot longer if you get it regular tune-ups. An oil change, tires rotated, check on the gauges, align the front end. And you'll last a lot longer if you keep your doctor's appointments. A check-up, blood pressure reading, cholesterol measure—you know the drill. Now, just do the same thing with your Target Filter!*

www.thewhalehunters.com

# Ten Tweaks for Your Target Filter

In a turbulent economy, big companies are changing more rapidly than usual.  Some companies are retrenching to preserve cash and weather this storm:  slashing budgets, closing locations, consolidating departments, laying people off, reducing their scope of products and services. Other companies are taking advantage of a slow economy to seize opportunity:  modifying their business strategy, investing in new products or services, acquiring competitors, hiring from an excellent applicant pool, increasing their marketing and R&D budgets.

Regardless of how the whales are responding, they are likely not the same company they were the last time they made it through your target filter and on to your whale chart.  They may have totally new goals, new rules and reasons around their buying decisions, different expectations, different decision-makers, different time-frames to produce ROI.  Your job, as always, is to know everything you can learn about your targeted whales–to know far more than your competitors know.

**Quick review:** Your Target Filter is the set of criteria by which you determine an ideal large customer for your company.  (See Volume I). It includes a set of categories that are important to you and metrics for each category.  Categories include things like company size, location, industry, brand, corporate structure (e.g. public, private, government, or nonprofit)

Here's a Target Filter Tune-Up Checklist:

1. With your team, brainstorm the characteristics of your best big customers from the past three years.  Do you still want more customers like those?  If so, be sure those characteristics match up with your Target Filter.

22

2. Have your products or services changed since you last reviewed your Target Filter?  Do you have plans to enter a new market, a new industry vertical or a new geographic location, for example?  You may need a separate target filter for that industry or that product.

3. What's new in your industry?  What market trends are you observing?  Test your Target Filter to be certain it is up to date.

4. Ask your Scout to update dossiers on your Whale Chart list.  Do those whales still meet your criteria?  If not, remove them and find new ones that now meet your criteria.

5. Have you implemented Whale Signs?  These are signals of a prospect's potential readiness to buy.  You should subscribe to RSS feeds or set Google alerts to learn anything new that is going on with the whales on your Whale Chart.  Review your Whale Signs to be certain that you have identified the best ones for you.

6. What are you learning during your sales process?  Are you still well-aligned with what prospects want, or are you finding gaps that you didn't find before?  The target filter needs to lead you to companies that want what you have to sell.

7. Are you consistently getting bigger sales and bigger customers?  If not, or if your sales process has stalled, your target filter is no longer working for you.

8. Have you involved your entire team in the target filter discussion?  The perspectives from operations, customer service, and the key account management team are very important. Build consensus among sales and operations about the target filter criteria and metrics.

23

9. Is your target filter realistic?  If your vision of an "ideal client" never materializes in your sales process, you may have a pipe dream rather than a filter.

10. Do you allow your target filter to remind you when to say no to an opportunity that comes your way, such as an unsolicited RFP or a customer referral?  Unless these unexpected opportunities are consistent with the Target Filter, you should be confident about saying no.

The Target Filter is a critically important tool for whale hunting companies.  By developing a solid filter, reviewing and tuning up regularly, and sticking to the prospects who meet its criteria, you will close more sales, bigger sales, and better sales, routinely.

Learn more about "charting your waters"–using the tools of scouting (Target Filter, Whale Chart, Whale Signs, Dossiers) in *Whale Hunting: Land Big Sales and Transform Your Company*, available from amazon.com.

Visit our website now to claim your free infographic How Team Selling Lands Bigger Customers, Bigger Deals!
http://thewhalehunters.com/infographic1

# Reflection

In the following chart, make notes about each of the "10 Tweaks" and whether or not you have work to do on any of them. Do this with your team if you can.

| | |
|---|---|
| **Tweak 1** | |
| **Tweak 2** | |
| **Tweak 3** | |
| **Tweak 4** | |
| **Tweak 5** | |
| **Tweak 6** | |
| **Tweak 7** | |
| **Tweak 8** | |
| **Tweak 9** | |
| **Tweak 10** | |

info@thewhalehunters.com

www.thewhalehunters.com
© 2007-2016 The Whale Hunters, Inc.

# Action

In this chart, make note of specific action items that you want to create related to your comments on the Reflection chart. Identify the responsible person and the due date for each action item.

| Item | Action | Person Responsible | Due Date |
|------|--------|--------------------|----------|
| Tweak 1 | | | |
| Tweak 2 | | | |
| Tweak 3 | | | |
| Tweak 4 | | | |
| Tweak 5 | | | |
| Tweak 6 | | | |
| Tweak 7 | | | |
| Tweak 8 | | | |
| Tweak 9 | | | |
| Tweak 10 | | | |

26

*When it comes to parties, "the more the merrier," right? And so it can be in business collaboration, too. You can not only improve effectiveness but streamline your collaboration as well by following our 10 acceleration practices.*

27

# Fast Times

Acceleration. It's the difference between a 4-cylinder Civic and a V-8 Jag. Both can cruise at highway speeds, but only one can gain more speed while it's already moving fast. In the business world, the desire to move faster often causes management to exercise more central control. One foot on the gas, one set of hands on the wheel, one eye on the road, and one on the rear view mirror. It's a one-person show – too risky to share.

Yet think of how high-performing racing teams create speed by collaboration. The precise tuning of the chassis, the engine, the tires; the intense communication between the driver and the crew Chief; the orchestrated efforts of the pit crew. These teams prove that acceleration and collaboration go hand-in-hand.

Accelerating collaborative teamwork is a core promise of whale hunting. When a company is trying to cross No Man's Land (see Volume I) increased speed is essential. Yet increased collaboration is equally important. Whenever a boat brings a whale to the beach, the village needs to increase its speed of work immediately. Excuses, rationales, reasons – they pale against the reality of a ready whale on the beach for harvest.

But one of the hardest problems our clients face is to accelerate their processes, especially when they are trying to involve many people. Everyone buys the promise of moving faster. Almost everyone wants to accelerate their learning and implementation of promising new processes that will increase their sales, delivery, revenue, and profits. And they tout the benefits of collaboration – buy-in from the team, preparing the next generation of managers, knowledge sharing, and building best practices.

www.thewhalehunters.com
© 2007-2016 The Whale Hunters, Inc.                    info@thewhalehunters.com

Yet the burden of the everyday routinely sabotages the acceleration plan. We get mired in "how we do things." Meetings, checks and balances, approvals, reports, circulation of every plan to everyone. Collaboration seems too clunky, too hard, too slow. So a few people take over, and others step back. When that happens, the village is not ready for whales.

If you want to energize your progress through speed and collaborative decision-making, you need to streamline your collaboration tactics. Here are 10 practices to move forward fast:

1. **Define the purpose.** The only reason to collaborate across departmental or divisional lines is to increase the likelihood of good decision-making. Collaboration isn't about keeping everyone informed about everything. It's about getting the right information to the right people at the right time so that the organization makes decisive judgments based on collective knowledge.

2. **Keep moving.** Set the schedule of meetings, events, and deliverables upfront. The desire for a face-to-face meeting represents the biggest procrastination excuse for a collaborative team. Is there ever a time when all members of a 12- or 20-member cross-functional team can promise to be present? Very likely NOT! Keep to the schedule regardless of who cannot attend. Send someone in your place. Bring one another up to speed. But don't slow the process.

3. **Use an online communication space.** Share ideas, working papers, comments, drafts, and concerns in an online discussion: a web-based or server-based solution, a simple email bulletin board, or an internal service. Many useful technologies are available to support information-sharing among people who have difficulty being in the same place at the same time.

info@thewhalehunters.com

www.thewhalehunters.com
© 2007-2016 The Whale Hunters, Inc.

4. **Be here now.** When you are with your team, recognize what a precious time that is. Be there totally with your full attention (no email, cell phones, multi-tasking). Show up on time. Be prepared.

5. **Meet only to DO work.** Meetings are not for reporting, presenting, or sharing. They are ONLY for reaching decisions based upon previously shared materials. Circulate reports ahead of time. Share ideas in a chat room; brainstorm via email. Assign someone to organize the findings. Then come together to act on what you've learned.

6. **Focus on the future.** Shared understanding of the past is both impossible and irrelevant. How many meetings digress to a rehearsal of past attempts, failures, and shortcomings? A fast collaborative team is driven by a powerful shared vision of how good things are going to be when we get this next bit of work completed. Don't short-change the future by re-hashing the past.

7. **Build and test models.** Models are representations of "the real thing." They have the characteristics of the system you are trying to build on a smaller, cheaper scale. Simulations, games, process charts, 3-D versions, analogies, drawings – all of these models allow you to test ideas, processes, and practices before you implement.

8. **Communicate frugally.** Send information promptly to key teams whose work is affected by your progress. Focus on the commitments (who agreed to do what, in what timeframe) and the action items (what needs to happen next). Don't glut the system with extensive minutes and meeting notes that no one will read. Just the lack of time to produce minutes is a detractor to acceleration.

www.thewhalehunters.com
                    info@thewhalehunters.com

9. **Embrace progress, not perfection.** Think again of that racing team. They measure progress in a quarter-turn of the wrench, a .10 increase in speed, a one-step quicker tire change. Everything that they deal with is variable; they are in a constant flux to get the most speed out of their driver and their equipment under a given set of conditions, most of which are beyond their control (heat, rain, inspection lines) and changing by the day, hour, and minute. Take one step ahead today; take another step ahead next week. You don't need to do it all at once.

10. **There is no They.** We have sat through countless painful, unproductive meetings in which every proposed action was impeded by the phrase, "They'll never approve that." Or, "We can try it, but they'll shoot it down." "They" may be managers, employees, other departments, customers, board members – you name it. "They" are in charge. And because "they" are in charge, "we" let ourselves off the hook of decisiveness. What could your committee / task force / team / leadership group accomplish if you simply assumed that "they" are "you"?

Visit our website now to claim your free infographic How Team Selling Lands Bigger Customers, Bigger Deals!
http://thewhalehunters.com/infographic1

info@thewhalehunters.com                    www.thewhalehunters.com
© 2007-2016 The Whale Hunters, Inc.

# Reflection

What habits does your team have that slow down your progress? Get some people together and brainstorm. Then evaluate each one from (1) Minor Annoyance to (5) Big Problem.

| Slow-down Habit | Evaluations Score 1-5 |
|---|---|
|  |  |
|  |  |
|  |  |
|  |  |
|  |  |

32

# Action

Select three habits that were scored 3 or higher on the scale of minor annoyance (1) to big problem (5).

With your team, figure out a strategy to deal with each problem habit. Put someone in charge of progress, and set a date to eliminate!

| Problem Habit | Strategy to Eliminate | In Charge | Elimination Date |
| --- | --- | --- | --- |
| | | | |
| | | | |
| | | | |

33

www.thewhalehunters.com
© 2007-2016 The Whale Hunters, Inc.

*The most successful whale hunters are the ones who involve their team in a large, complex sale. Big company buyers want to meet and evaluate the capabilities of the people they'll be working with and depending on for these services, so you need ways to trust your team enough to turn them loose in a sales situation. Here's how!*

# Who Do You Trust?

Groucho Marx and Johnny Carson each hosted an old game show called "Who Do You Trust?" The contestant had to decide whether to answer the question himself or hand it off (in those days!) to his wife or another female co-contestant. Decades later, we played the same game in Jeff Foxworthy's "Are You Smarter than a Fifth-Grader? and Meredieth Vieira's "Who Wants to Be a Millionaire?" The whole premise is how and when to trust others to help you win.

Likewise in whale hunting, you will increase your odds of winning if you learn to trust your team. We have hammered the point that whale hunting is a team sport, and I know you believe it. But when you get close to the big win, it is oh-so-tempting to do the deal yourself—whether you are the chief, the shaman, or the harpooner. Nevertheless, the buyers' table wants to get close to your subject matter experts [SMEs] on a peer-to-peer basis. IT, financial, engineering, customer service—anyone will be affected by a decision to do business with you—expects a professional performance from your team.

You've read probably all there is to read about the art of delegation. But if you are still struggling to really trust your team to land the whale, what can you do about it? Here are five principles that can help.

Teach. You can't trust a team that doesn't know what to do or how to do it. So you have to invest in their training. We've described the concept of "power your boat"—that is, ensure that each subject matter expert is equipped with a set of power questions, power tools, and power points. Not only do they need to have the content down pat, but they need to consider what the give-and-take will be like and the ways in which they will interject their key points. Your team members need explicit guidance about the scope of their role, when they are to speak, and when they are finished.

**Rehearse.** You can teach and train in the abstract, but nothing substitutes for the dress rehearsal. Do a complete run-through, with other employees role-playing the members of the whale's buying team. Give your people the opportunity to field questions and to receive constructive feedback on their performance. Don't leave to chance the simple principles of being on time, dressing appropriately, turning off the cell phones, giving a firm handshake. Behaviors that are second-nature to an out-in-front person may be foreign to your people who normally work behind the scenes. They cannot make good decisions about concepts and details that they don't really know or understand.

**Direct.** Trusting your team doesn't mean abandoning your leadership role. Help to set the stage. Explain why this whale is important and why the village has invested in the hunt. Let everyone know why they have been selected to participate and what value they can bring to the exchange of information with the whale. Be specific about your expectations—that your team will be prepared, that they will represent you in an appropriate professional manner, and that they will follow the script that you have mutually determined. Make it clear that you will monitor the performance, whether or not you actually participate in a particular meeting or event.

**Measure.** Reinforce your leadership expectations with detailed metrics. These may range from an informal debrief immediately following a meeting to an ongoing system to measure performance—process steps completed, movement to the next step demonstrated, deals pitched, deals closed—and deals that your team walks away from, with confidence. Everyone on the boat needs to understand how their personal contributions will be evaluated and by what means they will be supported in learning and improving. Subject matter experts seldom have thought

36

of themselves as part of a sales team. They may be fearful or even resentful of "sales" at the outset.

Reward. If you want a powerful cross-functional team representing you in front of a whale's buying team, you'll need to reconsider their incentives. Maybe it's not only the harpooner who is rewarded with commission for a sale. As you develop trustworthy subject matter experts who can fulfill their roles gracefully, you can expect to see your sales results improve. The SMEs need to share in the wealth that a new whale brings to your village, not only through their normal, everyday roles but through their new learnings and cross-functional assignments.

Who Do You Trust? If you teach, rehearse, direct, measure, and reward, you can develop over time a trustworthy team—as we call them, a boat—to hunt and help to harvest new whales. Resist the temptation to answer every challenge yourself and you will unlock powerful new capabilities in your enterprise.

www.thewhalehunters.com
© 2007-2016 The Whale Hunters, Inc.

# Reflection

### Teach, Rehearse, Direct, Measure, and Reward

For each of the five ways you can become more trusting of your team to participate in a sale (or to undertake any other important task that you haven't delegated), identify who could benefit from this method (one or more people) and why.

| Activity | Who Could Benefit | Why |
|---|---|---|
| Teach | | |
| Rehearse | | |
| Direct | | |
| Measure | | |
| Reward | | |

38

# Action

Select three people whose names are on your previous list and identify your plan to better prepare them so you will feel more trust in allowing them to participate in customer-facing situations.

| Name | Activity | Detail | When |
|------|----------|--------|------|
|      |          |        |      |
|      |          |        |      |
|      |          |        |      |

www.thewhalehunters.com
© 2007-2016 The Whale Hunters, Inc.

*Sailors through the ages have fought to keep barnacles at bay – otherwise their vessels' performance would falter. To keep your company ship-shape, you've got to recognize and then keep your "barnacle behaviors" under control, too.*

40

# Fighting Barnacles

From the ancient Inuit umiak to the George H.W. Bush CVN-77 aircraft carrier, barnacles have been nothing but trouble for boats.

You know barnacles. They're passive predators that attach to the bottom of your boat and interfere with its performance. In its larval form, a barnacle has to locate a permanent environment that appears to be safe – or else it will die. When it picks a suitable spot, often the bottom of a boat, the larva fastens itself headfirst to the surface. If not forcibly removed, it is cemented to that surface for the rest of its life. And it grows. It brings its friends and neighbors along and they grow, too.

The resulting mass causes boats to lose speed and maneuverability, so wise sailors for centuries have been careful to keep their boats moving, lift them out of the water when not in use, and scrape barnacles from the hull when prevention fails.

When you launch a boat to hunt a whale, you can't afford to carry barnacles with you. We define barnacles as dissonant employees and their behaviors that grow, attract others, and disrupt the course and speed of your boat. For a successful hunt, you will need to keep them from attaching to the boat, or scrape them from the bottom of the boat, as soon as you recognize them.

How can you recognize the barnacles? Here are four versions:

The Camouflage Barnacle. These barnacles are bright and attentive during meetings and vocally supportive of whatever you suggest. If asked about the project's feasibility, they will respond, "Yes, that is certainly possible." Sometimes they have positions of authority within the hunt. They always seem to be working,

41

often cheerfully, on whatever project you've given them. They attend meetings, develop charts, and present reports.

Yet their part of the hunt never seems to move forward. Or parts of it will move forward, but the whole is never connected. They manage to make known throughout the company that others are preventing them from completing the hunt.

They are extremely hard to spot and can only be identified by their behaviors, not by outward appearances. Yet they are still barnacles and therefore immensely destructive. They present themselves as part of the boat and can remain there for many years, slowly but surely keeping the whale hunting process from being sharp, clear, and successful.

The Cheapskate Barnacle. Another barnacle is the employee who believes the cheapest is always the best. This employee will gripe about the amount of money being spent to hunt whales. She will point out to her co-workers things that could have been purchased with the money being expended. She will predict failure and will remark about the time being wasted on a losing cause.

You may hear her say, "Just send that money to my department and see what we can do with it!"

Only a small amount of time is needed for this kind of complaint to attach itself firmly to the boat and attract others. Rumors will begin to float that raises will be smaller this year because of this whale hunt. Resources will be constrained. Soon there will be many conversations in the hallways that begin like this: "Yeah, I think this is a wonderful project, but..." or, "It would be wonderful if this could really happen, but..."

**The Way We Were Barnacle.** The third type of barnacle adopts the role of unofficial historian and keeper of the culture. He will say, "That's not the way we've always done it," or, "That's not how we do it here." As your company takes up whale hunting as a deliberate strategy, you will make changes in how you conduct business. A whale hunt is not the usual kind of sale. And the ways that have worked in the past are not going to work in this instance. Change is difficult although necessary. This employee, however, takes change as a negative reflection on what has been going on in the company. He does not understand that the accomplishments of the past have created your current whale hunting capacities. He prefers hunting seals and mistrusts anything out of the ordinary. He expresses his nostalgia for earlier days and longs for those days when:

- "The CEO knew everyone in the company by name."

- "We had personal relationships with our customers, not such business-like ones."

- "We didn't take such risks."

- "We didn't all have to be involved in sales."

- "We were like a family and weren't so wrapped up in making money. We loved just making our widgets."

**The Doomsday Barnacle.** The final type of barnacle is the employee who sees herself as the custodian of past failures. As whale hunting is introduced, this employee's response is, "We tried that once before, and it didn't work." Never mind

info@thewhalehunters.com

www.thewhalehunters.com
© 2007-2016 The Whale Hunters, Inc.

that times, employees, attitudes, possibilities, knowledge, markets, and even the company itself have all changed since then. This employee is so fond of her position that she will willingly tell anyone – who will stand still and listen – of the many efforts that have been made in the past to do this very thing… and how they have all failed. The more spectacular the failure, the more she delights in her retelling of it.

### Barnacle Control

If you are going to launch a whale hunt, be scrupulous about maintaining your boat. Watch for barnacles and do not allow them to attach themselves. If you discover barnacles on the hull, be diligent in removing them.

It is not productive to try to change employee attitudes, but when those attitudes lead to behavior – and that includes vocal behavior – that threatens the boat's maneuverability, they must be scraped from the boat.

Prevent barnacles by refusing to provide a safe haven for them. Your associates and employees can point to "barnacle behavior" with unfailing accuracy. They are watching to see if you recognize the same characteristics that they observe. And most important, they are watching to see if you will preserve your boat or threaten its safety by permitting barnacles to make it slow and clumsy.

Commit to a barnacle-free boat, and whale hunting success will follow.

# Reflection

Here's an activity to do by yourself or with your most trusted advisors. Do you have people on your team with "barnacle" behaviors?

Start by identifying comments that you hear that reflect barnacle thinking:

_____

_____

_____

_____

_____

_____

_____

Then, identify whether these comments are widespread among your team or usually come from only one or two people?

_____

_____

_____

_____

_____

_____

_____

info@thewhalehunters.com          www.thewhalehunters.com
© 2007-2016 The Whale Hunters, Inc.

# Action

**Step One.** If you observe barnacle behavior(s) among many people on your team, identify each of those behaviors and determine one way you could make it stop:

| Name | Due Date |
| --- | --- |
|  |  |
|  |  |
|  |  |

**Step Two.** If you have any individual on your team who behaves like a barnacle routinely, determine how you are going to fix the problem. Seek advice from your board, mastermind group and/or executive team if you are not sure what to do.

*Hail to the Chief... Executive, that is, who joins the whale hunt! But only to the Chief who is used judiciously, appropriately, and regularly – and who is adequately prepared to perform this critical role.*

47

# The Chief in the Boat

William Shatner has been typecast throughout his career in such roles as Captain James T. Kirk, T.J. Hooker, Denny Crane on Boston Legal and most recently as a nosy dad in a Priceline commercial. His character is always a genius, a wildcard, a strategist, a nightmare – and completely unpredictable.

William Shatner's characters are like many CEOs we encounter. What do you do when the CEO as Chief of the Village decides to get on the boat to join the whale hunt?

The Chief in any village is the source of ultimate decisions. His power, her authority come from wisdom, fierceness in the face of adversity, accumulated knowledge of what works and what doesn't, and the ability to outlast the competition. CEOs become nervous when their companies are hunting whales, and they feel those nerves can only be calmed by getting involved in the hunting process. Many companies choose to engage the CEO as part of the pursuit team but attempt to manage around the CEO's natural inclinations for fear of the uncontrollable variable that he or she can be. As a valuable asset, your CEO needs to be used judiciously, appropriately, and regularly.

1. **Use your Chief judiciously.** It is not just a matter of respect to choose the proper pursuit for your CEO; it is also an issue of allocating resources wisely. If the CEO is engaged in opportunities that are too small, she will lose interest in the prospect and question the pursuit's legitimacy. If the CEO is engaged in dialog with a junior person, it may imply to the client that you are a small firm or that the CEO micro-manages the work to the point of ineffectiveness. If the CEO is engaged too early, it may give the appearance that the piece of business has more weight to the future of your firm than you want to relay to your prospect. Pay close attention to these factors.

48

- **Right size of opportunity.** Ask your CEO to engage in opportunities that are truly whales. The Whale Hunters define a whale as an opportunity which is 10 to 20 times the size of your average account. If your CEO is spending time discussing, strategizing about, or meeting with opportunities which are not of this size, you are wasting his time.

- **Right level in the organization.** There is a popular idiom in management circles these days called "top-to-top" meetings. Your CEO should be meeting with the most important economic driver in your prospect's firm. Often the person in the "C"-suite, with responsibility for finance, operations, marketing, sales, or the Chief executive herself, meets this criterion. However, title is not the deciding factor for including your CEO; rather, buying power and authority should determine her involvement. This calculation can be difficult, but for your CEO to be involved, seek the person ultimately responsible for the strategy decisions in your prospect's area of interest. The strategist is often the person with the ultimate accountability for success and failure of your work. Your CEO and this person have ultimate accountability in common, and therefore a partnership between the two of them makes sense.

- **Right time in the process:** Too early or too late defines bad timing for CEO involvement. The CEO should be involved on schedule, which is another way of saying, "on purpose." While crafting a plan to pursue a whale, your team should have a natural point outlined well in advance for CEO attendance at a meeting. It is a mistake to involve the CEO without the proper "signs" from the client; it's also a mistake to bring the CEO in "off-plan."

info@thewhalehunters.com

www.thewhalehunters.com
© 2007-2016 The Whale Hunters, Inc.

2. **Use your Chief appropriately.** The few meetings in which the CEO is included have real sales power if managed properly. As the Chief of the Village, the CEO has to demonstrate to the prospect that she has pride in her organization and faith in its ability to deliver on promises. Additionally, the CEO must add the power of his position through personal commitment to the potential client. The CEO should share his insight, creativity, and institutional memory to add value to the client.

- Faith. A demonstration of the CEO's pride and faith in the organization is crucial to the sales process. Without strong internal belief from the top down, it will be impossible for the prospect to share in that belief and make a positive decision about your company.

- Commitment. In meetings the CEO must visibly demonstrate a personal commitment to the whale. This commitment can be in the form of a promise (with delivery) of follow-up calls, involvement in installation or start-up, or other tangible proofs of ongoing participation.

- Insight, Creativity, and Institutional Memory. In "top-to-top" interaction, it should be the hope of every boat to develop relationships of mutual respect and potential friendship. Your CEO can help a client avoid missteps, approach problems from a different perspective, and think strategically about potential issues.

info@thewhalehunters.com

3. **Use your Chief regularly.** The CEO is neither the boat member of first choice nor last resort. However, regular use of your CEO should be about a predictable whale hunting process in which the role and timing of the CEO's involvement have been determined very early in the process. Sporadic involvement of the CEO demonstrates to prospects a clear lack of integration with the team during meetings and hand-offs. A scheduled use of the CEO reduces the whale's anxiety. It's also instrumental in organizational understanding of the whale hunting process, the life cycle of the sale, and the need for a full boat for large pursuits.

- Predictable. CEOs do not like surprises – for good reason. A surprise usually points to a lack of information or planning on the part of a team. Whale hunting is a process, not an event. Therefore, knowing how and when the CEO will be engaged should be easy to determine early in the hunt.

- Integration with the team. A team functions well through repeated drills and the muscle memory created by sustained and repetitive interaction. Simply to rehearse looking like a team will not make you a team. The CEO needs a predictable and repeated role in the whale hunting process so that the organization will improve its ability to hunt together.

- Understanding of the whale hunting process. Whale hunting is unique, and the process is different for your organization from typical sales efforts. For these reasons, the process can be confusing to the CEO, even after much education. Allowing the CEO to be part of the boat regularly reminds him that whale hunting is important, it takes time, a lot of people are involved, and the return can be extraordinary.

A caveat on price negotiation

Many companies bring the CEO to meetings as the ultimate negotiator of price. This is a mistake on many levels. The CEO's role is to amplify the high value of your service offering. Putting the CEO in the position of marginalizing his own company's worth creates bad impressions and bad feelings. The CEO's role in setting price is behind the scenes, not in front of the prospect. Price decisions need to be made before or after the meeting and only relayed to prospects by the CEO as a matter of demonstrating personal commitment as outlined above. Using your CEO as the price negotiator during in-person visits weakens the team and guarantees future difficulties in client management.

Many organizations are uncomfortable with the role the CEO plays in the sales process. Part of this may be due to the CEO's personality. However, most fear relates to a lack of planning and agreed-upon expectations. It is our experience that clearly defined expectations, a process for predictable use of the CEO, and proper rehearsal, planning, and repetition are the formula components for successful hunts with the Chief in the boat.

Visit our website now to claim your free infographic How Team Selling Lands Bigger Customers, Bigger Deals!
http://thewhalehunters.com/infographic1

# Reflection

If you are the chief in your village, reflect on these questions:

1. How often do you participate in a large sale? Always? Often? Never?

2. Does your sales team manage how and when you will participate or do you tell them?

3. Does the whole team have a plan for your participation in a sale, or is your involvement sort of last minute and haphazard?

4. Would you prefer that your team handle your involvement in a different way?

If you are a salesperson or sales manager, reflect on these questions:

1. Do you ever involve your chief in a large sale?

2. Do you have the opportunity to invite your chief's participation or are you told to do that?

3. Are you satisfied that your company uses the chief most advantageously in your sales process?

4. Would you prefer to handle your chief's involvement in a different way?

info@thewhalehunters.com　　　　www.thewhalehunters.com
© 2007-2016 The Whale Hunters, Inc.

# Action

Looking at your answers to the previous page questions, what are the things that you would like to change about involving the chief in a sales process? Who would you need to involve in making that kind of change? Should this become a routine part of your whale hunting process?

| Change to Be Made | Who Would Need to Help | Insert Into Whale Hunting Process? |
|---|---|---|
| | | |
| | | |
| | | |
| | | |

*To sustain fast growth, a meritocracy is crucial. The guiding principle for a meritocracy is the assignment of value exclusively to performance. Six steps can help you expedite development of a meritocracy in your organization.*

# Are Fast-Growth Companies Meritocracies?

The Arctic North is a brutal environment with little room for error. Mistakes are not tolerated by the incredible cold and harsh climate. Whale hunting villages can ill afford to have members fail to bring back a whale, ignore or miss the signs of predators like wolves or polar bears, or be unready to act when all hands are needed. Life or death is an extremely efficient arbiter of merit.

For companies to sustain fast growth, a meritocracy is crucial. Firms that stall in their development can be weighed down by other forms of cultural management. But how do you shift from a "benevolent monarchy," or a "parliamentary" style of leadership, to one governed by individual performance? The first step is a clear definition. A meritocracy must meet certain requirements to warrant the designation. A meritocracy should be governed by the following:

- Clearly defined drivers of success for individuals and the organization

- Accountability attached to responsibility and vice versa

- Clearly understood consequences for both incidental and consistent failure

- Clearly understood rewards for meritorious performance

Firms that have grown quickly have often done so as a result of extremely hard work and loyalty. In the movie Castaway, a generational family of FedEx employees sits around the holiday meal recounting when Fred Smith and the team sorted the first deliveries by hand on card tables in a garage. This kind of kinship illustrates the way many firms feel about "the good old days."

Due to the needs of the business, fast-growth companies rarely start with what they see as non-essentials like personnel manuals, formal mentoring programs, clear individual performance, development plans, and so on. The theory is simple: "If we make it to the point that we are a real company, we will have the time to figure all that stuff out."

Unfortunately, the time for imposing the regimen and discipline of a more mature organization comes and goes, and the company remains committed to its "fast and loose" approach. Without the best people in the best positions to leverage their abilities, sustaining growth is very difficult. A guiding principle for a meritocracy should be assigning value based upon to performance, which is assessed objectively as possible. Such a process might look like this:

1. **Draft objective job descriptions for all positions.** Although this may seem obvious, the lack of written descriptions, including performance objectives, plagues many fast-growth companies.

2. **Determine the major leverage points in organizational performance.** Companies often look only to financial performance indicators. However, customer satisfaction, employee satisfaction, time to delivery, errors per thousand, and waste reduction are also important. Pick those factors that drive short- and long-term performance, and decide how each position contributes to those factors.

3. **Work with current staff to establish baseline expectations.** Benchmarking has been a key to all performance improvement. Establishing the metrics for current levels of performance will be difficult but necessary if this measurement does not already exist.

info@thewhalehunters.com

www.thewhalehunters.com
© 2007-2016 The Whale Hunters, Inc.

4. **Organize the company around an objective evaluation of personnel and company needs.** You need to avoid the mistake of reorganizing first, and then determining best fits. Take the time to follow the process systematically to avoid making mistakes in placement and definition.

5. **Communicate, communicate, communicate.** Change is difficult for everyone. Both the rationale for change and the expected improvement need to be clearly articulated.

6. **Recognize the value of each individual and his or her investment.** Too often, change in organizational structure as is contemplated here comes as a punishment for perceived failure. Restructuring a company to a meritocracy must avoid assigning blame by focusing on opportunity and fit.

Long-term employees and founding friends are important to the past and future of a firm. Separating the value of the past from the potential of the future will pay dividends for all involved. Fast-growth companies that follow a systematic approach to meritocracy development will shorten dramatically the time for such change to take place.

Visit our website now to claim your free infographic How Team Selling Lands Bigger Customers, Bigger Deals!
http://thewhalehunters.com/infographic1

# Reflection

What kind of "state" is your company today? Is it a monarchy, a benevolent dictatorship, a democracy, a republic, a meritocracy, or some other beast? Is it possible that some areas of your company focus and reward more based on merit than other areas?

Here are some questions that will help you reflect:

1. Do you have relevant, recent, widely-shared position descriptions for everyone in your employ?

2. Are your position descriptions sufficiently detailed to be used to evaluate performance?

3. Do you have a formal system of performance review that is widely understood and carried out consistently?

4. Do you consider a wide range of performance attributes in addition to bottom line contributions?

5. Do you give raises more or less "across the board" or do you use pay increased to reward the behaviors that you want to see among your employees?

info@thewhalehunters.com

www.thewhalehunters.com
© 2007-2016 The Whale Hunters, Inc.

# Action

If you agree with our thoughts about a meritocracy, make a list of five actions you could undertake that would move your company in that direction.

_____

_____

_____

_____

_____

_____

If you don't believe a meritocracy is what you want, make a list of five reasons to keep your current reward system.

_____

_____

_____

_____

_____

_____

60

*Fact, opinion, or gossip? By systematically sharing among your team what you know about your whales, you will transform common knowledge into shared knowledge and uncover new opportunities for growth as well.*

61

# Seeing Through the Fog

As a fast-growth company, yours has at least one whale among its current clients – a customer or account that is 10 to 20 times larger than average. But are you doing whale-sized business with each of your whales? Gaining new business within your key accounts is a very different process from scouting and harpooning new whales.

The Whale Hunters use the phrase "Searching for Ambergris" to describe the process of growing sales with your existing whale accounts. Ambergris is a rare substance produced only within the gut of a sperm whale. Used as a fixative for expensive perfumes and an aphrodisiac for kings, ambergris was for centuries considered to be more valuable than gold or precious gems.

The unknown areas of your whale are sources of ambergris for your company. Perhaps you deal with one division of a company but not with others. Or you may have regional operations but not a national contract. Possibly you are selling one of your products or services but not others. You need to know what you don't know! Unless properly managed, your knowledge and the whale's knowledge may inhibit the expansion of the whale account.

Why? Your whale believes that it knows you but may have your company slotted in a very narrow space, or in a space you no longer wish to occupy, or in a space you have outgrown. Likewise, your village believes that it knows your whale. But your villagers' whale knowledge may be limited to a particular buying group, division, or service area.

www.thewhalehunters.com
© 2007-2016 The Whale Hunters, Inc.                                    info@thewhalehunters.com

Each member of your team knows your whale in a different way. Personal relationships, functional responsibilities, and historical contexts all conspire to give each team member a different perspective. Use The Whale Hunters "Fact-Opinion-Gossip" exercise within your organization to help you transform "common knowledge" – that which you know individually – into shared knowledge.

Here's how it works.

- Bring your team together.

- Brainstorm a list of what you know about your whale that could affect your ability to dramatically grow your business in the next year.

- Then, "see through the FOG," labeling each statement FACT, OPINION, or GOSSIP.

- Discuss what you've learned and what you need to discover.

By "searching for ambergris," you can leverage common knowledge into shared knowledge, assess the culture of your whale and all of its buying groups, and develop strategies to grow business with your whale.

# Reflection

| What do we "know" about this customer | F Fact | O Opinion | G Gossip |
|---|---|---|---|
|  |  |  |  |
|  |  |  |  |
|  |  |  |  |
|  |  |  |  |

64

info@thewhalehunters.com

# Action

For all of the statements you labeled "Fact," how can that knowledge help or hinder you on your next sale?

_____

_____

_____

_____

For all of the statements you labeled "Opinion," how can you verify the statements? Which ones might be important to your next sale to this customer?

_____

_____

_____

_____

For any statements that you labeled "Gossip," do they relate to your ability to close a new deal with this customer? If so, how can you verify the statement and what will you do about it?

_____

_____

_____

_____

*Trust is at the heart of any good relationship, but it's particularly important to your relationships with whales. Integrate The Trust Cycle into your existing sales process to build stronger relationships and enjoy revenue growth as a result.*

66

info@thewhalehunters.com

# Growth Through Trust

What you capture is oftentimes not what you harvest. The Whale Hunters have discovered, for example, that relationships with new whale clients, which had initially appeared promising, sometimes produce only a fraction of what had seemed possible. These relationships fall apart for all sorts of reasons.

We teach The Whale Hunters Process™ to fast-growth organizations, providing them with the processes, roles, and skills necessary to bring in clients 10 to 20 times the size of their current average account. But what happens if a company has all the whales it needs to meet its goals and yet is unable to grow that business further? Another way by which we teach companies to fuel that revenue growth is called "The Trust Cycle."

Trust is at the heart of any good relationship. And stronger relationships with whales, developed quickly and effectively by all members of your team, help guarantee the path to revenue growth.

Why everyone? It's simple. Every employee who potentially "touches" your customer is critical to customer retention and the growth of your business. Yet many employees – those in such customer touch point functional areas as customer service, account management, and technical services, for example – balk at the idea of being called a "salesperson." But by integrating The Trust Cycle into your existing sales process, it's possible to achieve desired growth without trying to make everyone a salesperson.

info@thewhalehunters.com

www.thewhalehunters.com

Rules:

- The level of growth in a relationship is directly related to the level of trust at the touch points in your company.

- The level of trust in an account is dictated by the lowest level of trust at any one touch point. If you have five different people who regularly interact with an account, each of those people is a touch point. The person who generates the lowest level of trust represents the level of trust in your overall company.

- If you want to grow and protect an account, you must grow your trust.

It's important to understand that "lower levels of trust" do not necessarily mean that your whale "distrusts" you or feels your organization is "dishonest." If that were the case, you would more than likely be losing the business. That said, however, higher levels of trust pave the way for a growing relationship, a longer relationship, and the possibility of keeping a relationship even if you have aggressive competitors. That's why we advocate increasing trust so your company becomes more integrated into the fabric of your whale's company.

www.thewhalehunters.com
info@thewhalehunters.com

How do you build an organization that grows its trust with key customers? By increasing the capacity of each of your touch points to be "able" in the six elements of the trust cycle.

- **Connectable.** Create access to point of initial contact; determine interest and pain; explain your company's distinct value

- **Credible.** Credentialize efficiency, experience, expertise; anchor credentials to tangible references and cases; ask knowledgeable questions

- **Reliable.** Make and keep commitments; communicate impeccably; maintain confidentiality

- **Capable.** Deliver on brand; deliver on need; deliver to client's specifications

- **Likeable.** Like them first; create the sense of long-standing relationship; practice 100 details

- **Adaptable.** Understand the change environment and practice flexibility; adopt a long-term perspective; demonstrate empathy

To the degree that each of your company's touch points can understand the trust characteristics, the behaviors that generate trust, and clients' confirming behaviors, then your client relationships will grow and prosper. And, in growing whale clients, it's so much more about trust than it is about sales.

# REFLECTION

On the chart below, evaluate your company on the basis of each "ability" of Trust. Assume that "5" is the highest possible trust and "1" is very little trust at all. Do this with your team, if possible.

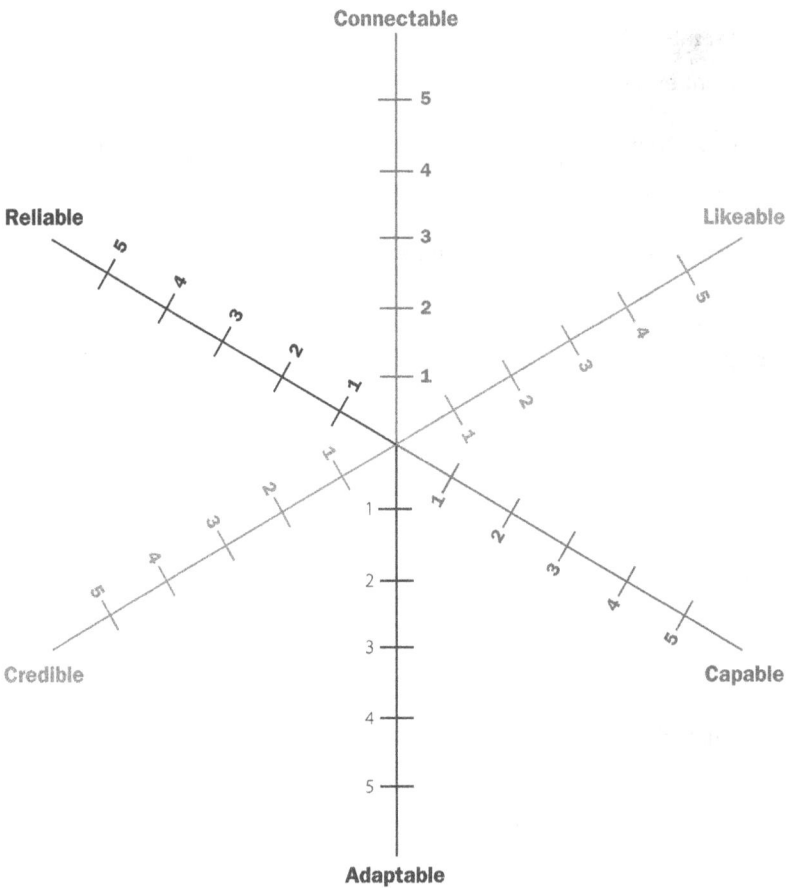

Connectable

Reliable

Likeable

Credible

Capable

Adaptable

70

# ACTION

On the same scale, reflect on your current level of trust with one of your largest customers, with "5" representing the highest level of trust and "1" representing not much trust at all.

With your team, have a discussion about whether your company is doing an excellent job of building trust with your customers; and, if not, what are the areas that you need to improve.

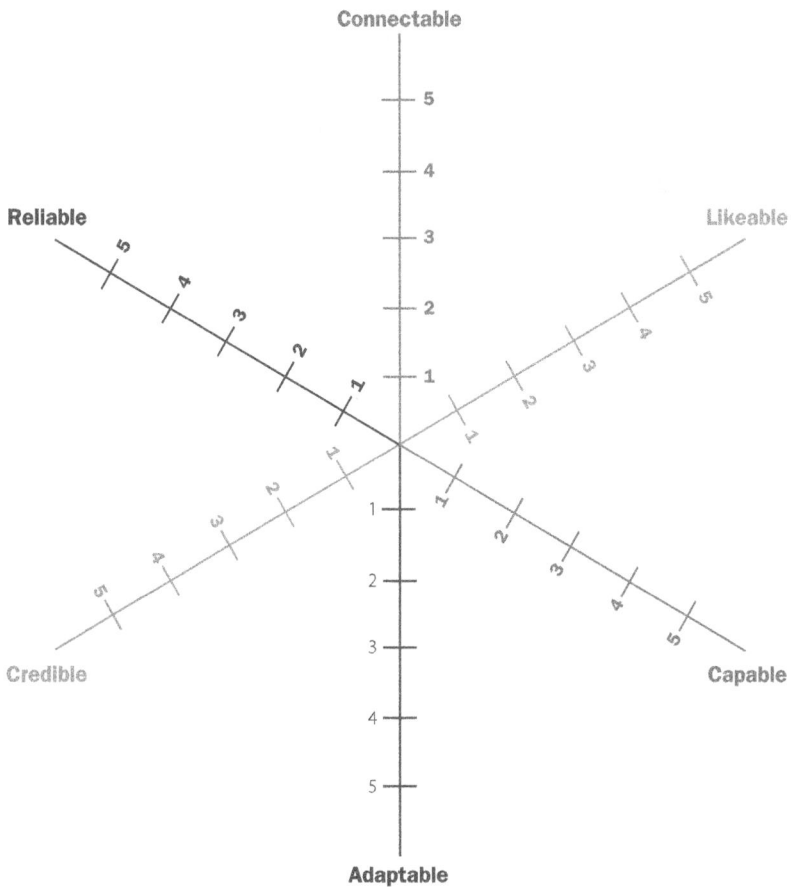

71

*No matter how hard you work to build trust, individuals can inadvertently damage trusting relationships. How does a whole company of generally trustworthy people behave like a trustworthy company? Here are some signs to watch for.*

www.thewhalehunters.com
© 2007-2016 The Whale Hunters, Inc.

info@thewhalehunters.com

# Trust Busters

Your boat worked hard to beach a new whale on the shores of your village. The members of your team deliberately built strong trust relationships with members of the buyers' table. So far, the whale trusts you, and you trust the whale. What can go wrong?

I'm writing about trust busters—behaviors by members of your team that can destroy the trust that you've worked so hard to build.

Here are the top five trust busters that can undo months of trust acceleration:

**Cold Hand-Offs.** Some boat members will no longer interact with this whale, while different people will join your team to service the whale account post-sale. Likewise, most of the buyers' table goes back to their regular assignments, and new people from the whale engage with you. How deliberately does your company handle these transitions? You have fantastic new opportunities to extend the trustworthy relationship with this whale, demonstrating integrity, openness, and investment throughout the process of fulfilling your contract. But your opportunities will depend on the strength of your internal communication of your team's commitments and the whale's expectations about what happens next. Who welcomes the whale to your village? How do you handle the next set of promises? The hand-offs from sale to contract fulfillment and the hand-off from fulfillment to customer service deserve your special attention on the trust spectrum.

**Personality Cult.** What happens when something goes wrong? If the whale gets upset early in a hand-off, chances are good that someone from the buyers' table will call a prominent person from your boat. "What's the matter with these guys," you will hear, "don't they know what you promised me?" Oh, what a temptation to be

info@thewhalehunters.com  www.thewhalehunters.com
© 2007-2016 The Whale Hunters, Inc.

the rock star! "I'm glad you called me," you want to say. "You just don't know how Finance operates here. They just don't get it. I'll be all over them – and next time, just call me first!"

**Us and Them.** As young companies grow, there's a real danger of tension between management and staff. Unlike the entrepreneurial, fire-fighting free-for-all, we're-all-in-this-together approach that got you up and running, the CEO and trusted advisors are now working hard to build a professional management team and take a more deliberate approach to doing business. In a mature company, the us vs. them distinctions may be legendary, fueling an active grapevine. In either case, some of this is inevitable and harmless. But when this attitude escapes to the whale, you're in trouble. "Well, I know they promised you a shipment in three weeks," someone says to your whale. "But they don't know what they're talking about! They don't know how many other orders we have, and they don't know how short-handed we are."

**Silos.** Departments and divisions can be notorious for ignorance of how the other functions. We've observed silos even in small companies, just because of the differences in responsibilities, roles, understandings, language and so forth that mark areas of expertise and specialty. Someone from the whale calls your project management department. "Hi, I'm John from XYZ Whale, and I'm calling to confirm that our training is scheduled for this date and time. Joan asked me to call and be certain that everything is in place and to find out what you need from us." What if the person who takes that call for you knows nothing about the training? What if she says, "I don't know what you're talking about. That's Training's business. I heard they're running behind."

What about Me. There may be people in your company who are reluctant to take responsibility. You've just completed a big installation, say a call center or an IT installation. A call comes in to the customer service. "My system is supposed to do XYZ, but it isn't working. I tried calling Operations, but they said you're responsible for this kind of issue." And what if your Help Desk person says, "They do that all the time. I haven't been trained on your system yet, but they just don't have the customer service attitude that we have."

Overcoming the Trust Busters.

We've identified five scenarios that are guaranteed to bust the trust you've cultivated with your whale. In every case, you want the person who speaks for your company to present a trustworthy "voice of the village." You'd like to be certain that no individual agendas or lack of understanding are getting in the way.

So here's how—four ways to improve your organization's ability to sustain and to grow the trust that your boat builds with the whale.

Intentionality. Make it a big deal. Be sure everyone knows about trust and how it works. Not in the abstract, but in the concrete details of the behaviors of integrity, openness, and investment. Help them to understand the personal, one-to-one role of every trust transaction, which represents the move from personal trust to organizational trust.

Training. See that everyone, at every level, can explain trustworthy behaviors, participate in scenarios where trust is at risk, and demonstrate how to respond in trust-accelerating ways.

**Collaboration.** Ensure that each department and division knows what the others do and understands their value to the enterprise.

**Reward Systems.** Link rewards to trust-building behaviors. Be ruthless about intolerance for internal finger-pointing, mixed messages, and lack of knowledge sharing. Highlight and reward behaviors that build trust internally and externally.

Chances are that almost everyone in your company is and wants to be a trustworthy person and a trustworthy employee. But how does a collection of trustworthy people become an organization that builds trust exceptionally well? We believe that if you train and reward to the behaviors of trust, you will build a priceless attitude about trust-building that will transform every one-on-one transaction with your whales as well as partners, allies, and friends.

Visit our website now to claim your free infographic How Team Selling Lands Bigger Customers, Bigger Deals!
http://thewhalehunters.com/infographic1

# Reflection

Alone or with your team, reflect on statements that people might make or things they might do that damage trust—especially when it was not their intention to do so. Document as many examples as you can.

_____

_____

_____

_____

_____

_____

_____

_____

_____

_____

_____

_____

_____

_____

_____

_____

_____

_____

_____

info@thewhalehunters.com                www.thewhalehunters.com
                                         © 2007-2016 The Whale Hunters, Inc.

# Action

Identify how each of these methods could help you create a team who are free of behaviors that tend to damage trust unknowingly.

Intentionality


Training


Collaboration


Reward System


Other?


Other?

# The Whale Hunters Glossary

The Whale Hunters draw upon the rich legend and lore of the Inuit whale hunters of the far northwest to engage executives in a new way of thinking: for explosive growth, hunt whales.

Ambergris - Rare and priceless substance produced deep within the gut of a sperm whale. The Whale Hunters use this term to represent additional value to be located within existing key accounts.

Beach - During the Beach phase (one of nine in The Whale Hunters Process™), you prepare and present the intake document, develop a harvest map, and commit to performance metrics.

Boat - The team of villagers who hunt and capture a specific whale. The team includes a harpooner, shaman, and several oarsmen, subject matter experts (SMEs) who are needed to close a complex sale. SMEs on each boat represent all areas of the company. The village Chief may also be involved.

Buyers' Table - Those at the whale company who will be affected by your company's solution and participate in the buying decision. Key positions at this table (among others) are the polar bear (economic buyer) and caribou (technical buyers).

Capture - The Capture phase, one of nine in The Whale Hunters Process™, involves those activities traditionally associated with "closing": finalizing the proposal, closing the deal, negotiating terms, and completing the contract.

www.thewhalehunters.com

Caribou - Individuals at the whale company - often technical buyers - who participate at the Buyers' Table and influence the buying decision; however, their position only allows them to say "no."

Chief - President, CEO, Founder or other person identified as responsible for the company's growth and delivery of profits. This person is responsible for ensuring that the village is ready to harvest whales, re-calibrates the Target Filter, and has final say as to whether a boat hunts or not.

Celebrate - During Celebrate (one of nine phases in The Whale Hunters Process™), your company conducts an internal post-harvest review, documents and integrates lessons learned, and determines ways to celebrate the whale (i.e. make the whale aware of both your company's appreciation for it and your company's commitment to your ongoing relationship).

Culture - The shared history of what has made your company successful. As the village transforms into a whale-hunting village, certain cultural beliefs change but core values can be maintained and reinforced.

Dossier (Scouting and Hunting) - Document used to communicate research information about a whale from the scout to the harpooner and shaman.

Eel - Gatekeepers, deal spoilers, and nay-sayers at the whale company who work to prevent any sort of change.

Gap Analysis - The results of an analysis the village performs comparing the needs of a particular whale against the village's current ability to meet those needs. Areas such as legal, finance, technology, operations, and logistics are typically included in such analyses.

Harpoon - Harpoon is one of the nine phases in The Whale Hunters Process™. During this phase, the whale hunter gets the whale's attention using a combination of an effective contact approach and a well-crafted message. Your company completes a needs assessment of the whale and designs and delivers a presentation to put forward your credentials and convey your understanding of the whale's needs.

Harpooner - Salesperson who hunts whales. The harpooner is responsible for identifying the key decision-makers inside of a whale, qualifying the whale, generating interest in the whale, and bringing the whale through the sales process.

Harvesting - This term refers to all activities that the boat and the village perform from the point of agreement with a client through a defined period of time (usually the first 90 days of the contract).

Honor - One of nine phases of The Whale Hunters Process™, Honor is the period of time surrounding that point when actual production or service delivery begins.

Intake and Setup - This term refers to specific activities the village and boat perform during the whale harvesting process. These activities are usually focused on an intense period of interaction just prior to the harvest through the first 30 days of contract performance.

Know - One of the nine phases of The Whale Hunters Process™, Know focuses on knowing your market, your strengths, your competition, and the ideal whales that you want to hunt.

Oarsmen - Key subject matter experts (SMEs) who are identified by the shamans and the village Chief to participate in the sales process on the boat. These individuals have specific knowledge of elements of the products/services that the company is selling and contribute to bringing the whale into the boat during The Whale Hunters Process™.

Polar Bear - Target decision-maker (also referred to as the economic buyer) at the whale company who can say "yes" or "no."

Process Map - Visual and narrative representation of the series of choreographed activities in the village's whale hunting process. It includes every element of the nine-phase process - from Knowing the Whale to Celebrating the Whale - in the detailed series of steps that are defined for a particular village.

Raven - Advocates of your company whose wisdom is sought after (and appreciated) by the shaman. Ravens take many shapes and forms. Some ravens are key insiders and associates of your company. Others are your guides on the customer side. Still another type of raven is a compensated intermediary.

Ride - During the Ride phase, you recruit and train subject matter experts to join your hunt, you analyze the whale's buying group, and you stage the whale's visit to your facility. Ride is one of nine phases in The Whale Hunters Process™.

Scout - Marketing person who performs research on whales, generates dossiers on whales, monitors the market for "whale sign," and supports the harpooners as per the shaman's direction.

Searching for Ambergris (SFA) - A specific process and set of tools for capturing more business with the village's existing whale accounts.

Seek - One of nine phases in The Whale Hunters Process™, Seek refers to the process by which your company collects, collates, and tracks account-specific information, including a prospect's readiness to buy. The shaman and harpooners use this information to decide which whales to hunt and how and when to hunt them.

Sew - This phase represents that time between a verbal or even contractual agreement to buy and the actual delivery of services. It is one of nine phases in The Whale Hunters Process™.

Shaman - The direct supervisor of a group of harpooners. The shaman is responsible for training the members of the boat, facilitating the whale hunting process, communicating with the tribe, and managing the tracking process.

Subject Matter Expert (SME) - Villager with responsibilities in hunting and harvesting a specific whale. SMEs represent such areas as research and development, legal, human resources, information technology, operations, manufacturing, shipping, and others. They are selected as oarsmen when a particular boat is launched.

Target Filter - The target filter is used as the evaluation chart for all prospective whales in the marketplace. Using the elements provided in the target filter, a score is given to each prospect whale and that score determines whether and when the village hunts.

The Whale Hunters Process™ - an integrated sales process by which a company is able to sell and service massive accounts.

Village - All members of the company in all departments.

Whale - A sales prospect for a company that is whale hunting. The prospect is distinct from other sales prospects because its meets pre-defined criteria of size and desirability as a client.

Whale Chart - Environmental scan of the marketplace and its inhabitants. This document identifies and qualifies the various opportunities in the marketplace by their desirable characteristics as a client.

Visit our website now to claim your free infographic How Team Selling Lands Bigger Customers, Bigger Deals!
http://thewhalehunters.com/infographic1

84

# Also Available from The Whale Hunters

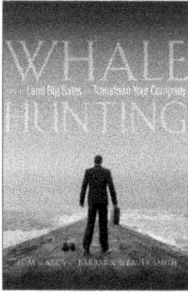

Whale Hunting is required reading for anyone who is going after the big fish in a market. Engaging, practical, and well organized, it is simply the best book on major account selling out there. Someone once said that confidence is going after Moby Dick in a rowboat and bringing the mayonnaise. *Whale Hunting* gives you the tools to pursue big deals with that kind of confidence.

~ Keith R. McFarland, author of *The Breakthrough Company: How Everyday Companies Become Extraordinary Performers*

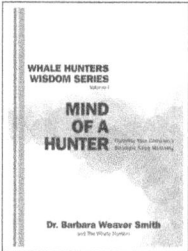

*Mind of a Hunter* reinforces the need for focus during a whale hunt. Each villager must know what each Inuit whale hunter knew: the whale is worth the trouble. No amount of distraction, fear, boredom, or nostalgia can be allowed to clutter the minds of the whale hunters eager to capture an account that will move your company to the next level.

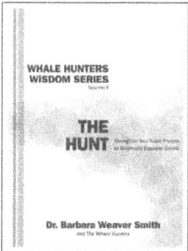

*The Hunt* introduces you to some of the unexpected ways a whale company can slip from the grasp of those small companies that are not able to hold the right tension on the harpoon line. Don't let the whale slip away from you. Learn the ways of the whale, the wind, and the water.

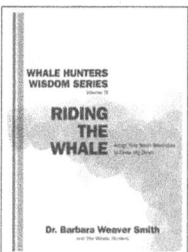

*Riding the Whale* explains why companies behave the way they do in the middle of your sales process and what you can do about it. In this volume, The Whale Hunters share their experiences and reflect on what it is like to ride the whale to successful completion of the hunt.

# Whale Hunting with Global Accounts: Four Critical Business Sales Strategies to Win Global Customers

*By Dr. Barbara Weaver Smith*

Discover the four critical sales strategies to win global customers, whether you're a seasoned global seller or just putting your toes into the ocean, a CEO or a sales manager. Featuring insights from interviews with fourteen global sales practitioners.

*"Barbara Weaver Smith does it again! In her new book, **Whale Hunting with Global Accounts: Four Critical Strategies**, she weaves in foundational concepts from her timeless book, **Whale Hunting: How to Land Big Sales and Transform Your Company** but adds a global bent. By capitalizing on the experience of fourteen experts (I was especially honored to be part of this elite group) she is able to analyze and address the many issues associated with landing and supporting global customers. If your company plans to expand your sales reach into global markets, I would suggest digesting every word of this book – it will save you countless hours and springboard your efforts to building a successful and sustainable global sales program."*

**WHALE HUNTING WITH GLOBAL ACCOUNTS**

Four Critical Sales Strategies to Win Global Customers

Foreword by Jill Konrath
**BARBARA WEAVER SMITH**

**Lisa D. Magnuson**
TOP Line Account™ Deal Coach
Top Line Sales

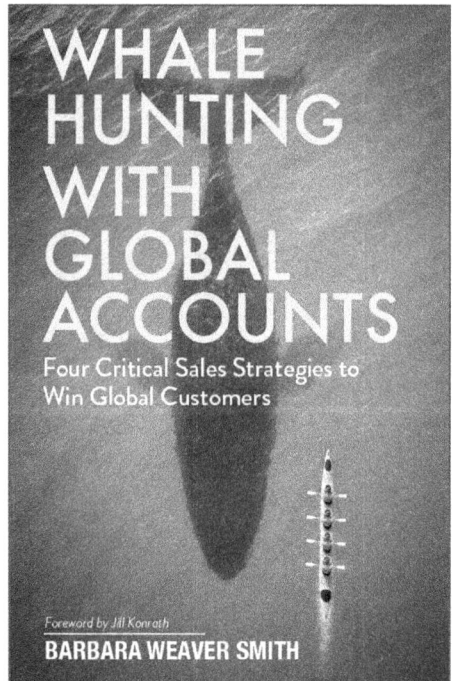

86

# Notes

# Notes

Visit our website now to claim your free infographic How Team Selling Lands Bigger Customers, Bigger Deals!
http://thewhalehunters.com/infographic1

Whale Hunters Wisdom, Volume IV: The Whale Hunting Culture

The Whale Hunters
3054 East Bartlett Place
Chandler, AZ 85249
www.thewhalehunters.com
info@thewhalehunters.com

Dr. Barbara Weaver Smith is available to speak to your organization about whale hunting, sales process development and integration, and accelerated cultural transformation. Contact The Whale Hunters at 480.584.4012 for more information.

www.ingramcontent.com/pod-product-compliance
Lightning Source LLC
Chambersburg PA
CBHW060636210326
41520CB00010B/1623